EBOLA

Understanding & Preparing for an Outbreak

Alex Smith

ISBN-13: 978-1502862020
ISBN-10: 1502862026

Note:

Other Works by Alex Smith

<u>Getting Home</u>

<u>Staying Home</u>

CONTENTS

Chapter 1: Introduction and Glossary

Introduction

Several months into the 2014 West African Ebola outbreak, I realized the information I had compiled was similar in breadth to the research I had previously done when writing my other books. It only made since to condense this information into book format, both for my use and your own.

This book has been written for the individual who has limited to intermediate knowledge regarding Ebola. It is written in a manner so as to not overwhelm you with unnecessary jargon or lengthy, technical descriptions of items. The goal is for this material to be short, concise and easily understood.

Relative to other diseases, not much is known about Ebola. Speak to an expert and they will undoubtedly tell you that, even still, something is *different* about the current outbreak. How this particular outbreak plays out is yet to be seen.

When writing, one typically has the benefit of reflection upon past events. We are able to use hindsight to parse the details. In this instance, however, we do not have that luxury. If the worst is realized, and we experience sustained outbreaks in the developed world, we will need the information beforehand.

Much of the information contained herein is open source. I have attempted to compile this information and present it in a format that is not overwhelming.

Caution: Much of the information contained herein should be left to trained professionals. Undertaking direct contact with a suspected Ebola victim puts your life in dire risk. This information is included for entertainment purposes only. In the event that a worst-case scenario is realized, and the virus overwhelms the authorities, you may be on your own for an extended period of time. This is not anticipated, however, fortune favors the prepared.

Again, this information is for entertainment purposes only. In all instances, contact the proper authorities immediately when an individual is suspected of being infected with the Ebola virus, or any life-threatening illness.

All information contained herein should be used at your own risk. I am not liable for any losses you may incur. Remember rule number one of dealing with an infected individual – avoid said individual.

Below I have included a glossary of terms that you will begin to hear in the news and read in this book. Understanding these terms is important. Refer back as needed.

Glossary of Terms

- <u>1:10 Bleach Solution</u>: 1 part household bleach (approximately 5% concentration) to 10 parts clean water. Produces a solution of approximately 0.5% bleach. Warning, caustic.

- <u>1:100 Bleach Solution</u>: 1 part household bleach (approximately 5% concentration) to 100 parts clean water. Produces a solution of approximately 0.05% bleach.

- <u>Airborne</u>: A disease that can be spread through the inhalation of tiny, dry particles that remained suspended in the air for long a period of time.

- <u>Airborne Droplet</u>: Relatively large, wet particles, propelled through the air by way of coughing, sneezing or violent vomiting that land on walls, floors, or other people.

- <u>Aerosol Transmissible</u>: A term advocated by the CIDRAP. Generally speaking, somewhere between Airborne and Airborne Droplet. Aerosol Transmissibles could be suspended in the air and carried by currents for an intermediate period of time. CIDRAP believes Ebola could be viable while suspended in the air for up to 90 minutes. The author is apt to agree with this possibility.

- <u>Asymptomatic Carrier</u>: An organism that has contracted an infectious disease, but displays no symptoms. Although they are unaffected by the disease themselves, they can transmit it to others. Also known simply as a carrier.

- <u>Basic Reproduction Number (R_o)</u>: Also known as Basic Reproductive Ration and Basic Reproductive Rate. Sometimes pronounced "R naught." The average number of people an infected person will in turn infect.

- <u>Biocontainment</u>: Containment of highly pathogenic agents (toxins, bacteria, viruses, etc.), typically in a laboratory setting.

- <u>Biosafety Level (BSL)</u>: The level of biocontainment required to isolate a biological agent in a facility. BSL-1 is the lowest rating. BSL-4 is the highest. Ebola is a BSL-4 rated virus. 11 BSL-4 facilities exist in the United States, though some of them typically operate under BSL-3 conditions.

- <u>Bush Meat</u>: The meat from wild game hunted for food in tropical environments. A suspected cause of initial infections.

- <u>Carrier</u>: See Asymptomatic Carrier.

- <u>CDC</u>: The Centers for Disease Control and Prevention. The national public health institute of the United States.

- CIDRAP: The Center for Infectious Disease Research and Policy. Not government affiliated. Part of the Academic Health Center at the University of Minnesota.

- Contact Tracing: The process of locating everyone who had close contact with infected individuals and monitoring them for a period of time to determine if they have been infected. 21 days is a common time period with Ebola.

- Endemic: An infection that is maintaining a steady state in a population. Infection rates are neither increasing, nor decreasing. For this to occur, the disease must have a Basic Reproduction Number (R_o) of one. Ebola is believed to currently have a rate of approximately one to two.

- Epidemic: A widespread occurrence of an infectious disease in a community at a particular time. For example, The West African nations of Liberia, Guinea and Sierra Leone are experiencing an epidemic.

- Epidemiologist: A health professional who investigates the patterns and causes of epidemics.

- Epizootic: Of, relating to, or denoting a disease that is temporarily prevalent and widespread in an animal population.

- <u>Exsanguination</u>: Blood loss sufficient to cause death.

- <u>Focus of Infection</u>: A place with the epidemiological factors needed for transmission of an infection. Examples may include daycares, airports, village wells, etc.

- <u>Fomite</u>: Any object or substance capable of carrying and transferring infectious organisms from one organism to another. Doorknobs, currency, clothing and skin cells are all examples.

- <u>Hemorrhage</u>: Fancy word for bleeding. Hemorrhaging can occur internally, where blood leaks from blood vessels inside the body, or externally, through the nose, ear, mouth, eyes, etc.

- <u>Hemorrhagic Fever</u>: Also known as Viral Hemorrhagic Fevers (VHFs). A diverse group of illnesses characterized by fever and bleeding disorders and all can progress to high fever, shock and death.

- <u>Hot Zone</u>: an area that is considered to be dangerous due to contamination be it chemical, nuclear, or biological. Monrovia, Liberia could be considered a current hot zone

- <u>Incubation Period</u>: The time elapsed between exposure and when symptoms become apparent. With Ebola, 2 to 21 days is the generally accepted incubation period, but is not the maximum. Also known as Latency Time.

- <u>Index Case</u>: Initial infected person. See Patient Zero.

- <u>Marburg Disease</u>: A VHF similar to Ebola. It was first noted during small epidemics in the German cities of Frankfurt and Marburg in the 1960s.

- <u>Martial Law</u>: Temporary measures imposed by authorities in the event of a disaster or other crisis when normal laws and measures fail to function effectively. Quarantines, curfews and warrantless searches and seizures may be enacted. Civil rights may be suspended.

- <u>N95</u>: National Institute for Occupational Safety and Health (NIOSH) rating for respirators and surgical masks that filter at least 95% of airborne particulates. The N indicates the mask is NOT resistant to oil. N95 is the most widely available and inexpensive mask of the three listed here. N-Series masks do not have a specified service life. They can be used as long they are not damaged or breathing resistances are not detected. Based on the number of healthcare worker infections, the author is of the opinion that N95 masks may not be of sufficient protection.

- <u>N99</u>: (NIOSH) rating for respirators and surgical masks that filter at least 99% of airborne particulates. The higher the efficiency, the more particulates the mask will filter out.

- <u>N100</u>: (NIOSH) rating for respirators and surgical masks that filter at least 99.97% of airborne particulates. The highest efficiency, and most expensive, mask.

- <u>Natural Reservoir</u>: The long-term host of a pathogen of an infectious disease. For Ebola, the natural reservoir is believed by many to be fruit bats. Also known as a nidus.

- Negative-Pressure System: an isolation technique used in specialized units within hospitals to prevent the spread of highly-infectious diseases. It includes a ventilation system that generates negative pressure to allow air to flow into the isolation room but not escape.

- Nidus: See Natural Reservoir.

- P95: (NIOSH) rating for respirators and surgical masks that filter at least 95% of airborne particulates. Resistant to oil. P-Rated masks are unnecessary for the purpose of protecting against infectious diseases. N-rated masks are sufficient for infectious diseases. P99 and P100 masks also exist.

- Pandemic: An epidemic of an infectious disease that has spread through human populations across a very large region. Multiple continents may be infected.

- Pathogen: Anything that can cause disease. An infectious agent.

- Patient Zero: The initial infected person. For the 2014 Ebola outbreak, patient zero is believed to be a 2-year-old boy from a village in Guinea. The child died on December 6, 2013. His mother died on December 13. A sister died on December 29. From there, it continued to spread. Also known as the index case.

- <u>PPE</u>: Personal Protective Equipment. Goggles, gloves, masks, protective clothing, etc. designed to keep one safe from injury, or in the case of Ebola, infection.

- <u>Quarantine</u>: Isolation.

- <u>(R_o)</u>: See Basic Reproductive Number.

- <u>Subclinical Infection</u>: An asymptomatic infection, resulting in an asymptomatic carrier. In 1906, Typhoid Mary was identified as having a subclinical infection of typhoid fever. She spent nearly three decades in forced quarantine, and ultimately died there.

- <u>Vector</u>: Any agent (person, animal or microorganism) that carries and transmits an infectious pathogen to another living organism.

- <u>Viral Shedding</u>: The expulsion and release of viruses following reproduction in a host. Shedding may be from one part of the body to another, or into the environment.

- <u>WHO</u>: The World Health Organization. A specialized agency of the United Nations that is concerned with international public health.

- <u>Zoonosis</u>: the process by which an infectious disease is transmitted between species. Bush meat is a zoonotic agent, and facilitates the transfer of Ebola from infected animals to humans.

Alex Smith

Chapter 2: General Information

Chapter 2 is divided into the following sections:

About

Strains

Symptoms

Transmission

When does a Person Become Contagious?

Diagnosis

Treatment

About

The Ebola Virus Disease (EVD) is one of several Viral Hemorrhagic Fevers (VHFs). Symptoms begin 2 to 21 days after exposure in 95% of infected individuals. Another 3% of individuals have symptoms that appear in the wider 1 to 42 day period. The incubation period for the remaining 2% have not been released. This translated to 1 in 20 infected individuals may have an incubation period outside of the normally advised 2 to 21 days.

1. Source: Are the Ebola outbreaks in Nigeria and Senegal over? Ebola situation assessment - 14 October 2014. World Health Organization. Web. Accessed 18 Oct. 2014‹http://www.who.int/mediacentre/news/ebola/14-october-2014/en/

2. Source: Haas CN. On the Quarantine Period for Ebola Virus. PLOS Currents Outbreaks. 2014 Oct 14. Edition 1. doi: 10.1371/currents.outbreaks.2ab4b76ba7263ff0f084766e43abbd89.

Symptoms can easily be mistaken for other diseases initially, as they are common to everything from the flu to malaria. This allows the virus a period of time for it to be spread before the infected are isolated.

As far as viruses go, Ebola kills its victims very quickly. It has a mortality rate of 25% to 90%, with a historical average of nearly 70%. Death by Ebola is horrific and is usually caused by dehydration or organ failure – specifically the liver and kidneys. While these traits are terrifying, they work against the disease. For a virus to spread, its hosts must be alive to spread it. Because of this, Ebola outbreaks have historically burned out quickly.

Strains

There are five known subtypes, or strains, of the Ebola
Virus. They are:

- Zaire Ebolavirus (ZEBOV): Discovered in 1976.
  Most lethal strain.

- Sudan Ebolavirus (SEBOV): Discovered in 1976.

- Ivory Coast Ebolavirus (ICEBOV): Discovered in
  1994. There has been only one known infection by
  ICEBOV. A scientist contracted the virus during the
  necropsy of an infected chimpanzee. He survived.

- Ebola-Reston (REBOV): Discovered in 1989 in Crab-
  eating Macaques (monkeys). REBOV is the only
  strain that is not known to cause infections in
  humans.

- Bundibugyo Ebolavirus (BEBOV): Discovered in
  2007. It is most closely related to the ICEBOV
  strain.

There are large variations between the strains
(approximately 30-40% variation between genome
sequencing). Because of this, if a vaccination is
developed for one subtype, it may not necessarily work
for the others.

Ebola is a virus only occurring in mammals, as best we know. Humans, monkeys, baboons, gorillas, chimps, pigs, dogs, fruit bats and other animals are known to be susceptible to the various strains. Different subtypes have differing effects on the species. In the instance of Reston, humans are asymptomatic, while can be fatal to monkeys. In other strains, fruit bats, dogs and other animals can be asymptomatic, while humans are left susceptible.

Sources conflict, but some believe that the 20 to 30 year-old age group appears to be particularly susceptible. This may be because this age group are the healthiest age group, and are more likely to be caring for the sick. Children would be more likely to be shielded from the disease, whereas their parents would be caring for infected family members.

Rates of genetic change are approximately 100 times slower than Influenza A, or approximately the same magnitude as Hepatitis B. It is not common for viruses to mutate methods of transmission, though it is possible.

Symptoms

Upon infection, Ebola targets the host's blood coagulative and immune defense systems. The attack on the coagulative system leads to hemorrhaging. The attack on the immune system leads to severe immunosuppression. Typically, symptoms of Ebola may appear anywhere from 2 to 21 days after exposure. The average appearance of symptoms is in 4 to 10 days.

Early symptoms (typically day 5 to 9):
- Severe headache (50% to 75% Patients) (Percentages shown where available)
- Fever (95%)
- Fatigue (85% to 95%)
- Sore muscles (50% to 80%)

Advanced symptoms (typically day 6 to 10):
- Fever (greater than 38.6°C or 101.5°F) (95%)
- Malaise
- Vomiting (~70%)
- Diarrhea (85%)
- Rash (15%)

Critical Symptoms (typically day 7 to 11):
- Brain damage
- Bruising
- Unexplained hemorrhage (bleeding or bruising) from the nose, eyes, mouth, anus, etc. (40% to 50%)

<u>Final Symptoms (typically day 8 to 12):</u>

- Seizures
- Loss of consciousness
- Massive internal bleeding
- Death (Historically 70%)

<u>Survivors Have Reported the Following Complications:</u>

- Bulimia
- Fatigue
- Headache
- Hearing loss
- Inflammation of the Parotid Glands
- Missed or Late Menstrual Periods
- Muscle and Joint Pain
- Tinnitus
- Swelling of the Testicles
- Tinnitus

Recovery may require months. Weight gain and strength recovery are slow. Ebola continues to be present for many weeks after resolution (months in semen).

Transmission

Ebola outbreaks are believed to start through a natural reservoir, such as a fruit bat. Other animals may feed on fruit dropped by the bat, or the bats themselves. It is believed that humans are infected through handling and consuming bush meat.

When an infection occurs in a human, Ebola can be spread in several ways. According to the CDC, Ebola is spread through:

- Direct contact: Direct contact (through broken skin or the nose, mouth, or eyes) with blood or other bodily fluids (such as saliva, urine, sweat, semen, breast milk, or feces) of the infected person.

- Animals: Natural reservoirs or carrier animals.

- Objects (fomites) that have been come in contact with the infected person:

Ebola can survive on fomites for various lengths of time, depending on environmental conditions. Laboratory experiments have shown that the virus can survive in infected tissue on surfaces for over 50 days at a temperature of 4°C (-15°F). In other experiments, the virus was able to survive in the dark for hours at temperatures of 20°C (68°F) and 30%-40% relative humidity. The amount of detectable virus was reduced to 37% of the original amount after 15.4 hours.

- ## Airborne droplets (Not Confirmed by Authorities):

The CDC makes no mention of transmission through airborne droplets in humans. Because of the severity of the current outbreak, however, transmission through airborne droplets seems like a possible explanation. Note that the author says <u>airborne droplets</u> and not simply <u>airborne</u>. There is a huge difference. Airborne implies that a disease can be spread through the inhalation of tiny, dry particles that remained suspended in the air for long a period of time. These particles could also theoretically be transferred through air currents. Ebola is not airborne in this sense. The rate of infection is much too low. If Ebola was truly airborne, it should spread at a rate similar to tuberculosis, chickenpox or measles. One person with measles, on average, infects 12 to 18 people. The current Ebola outbreak appears to spread, on average, to one to two people. This value is known as the Basic Reproductive Number, R_0. The following is a chart of the Basic Reproductive Numbers for various diseases.

Basic Repoductive Number Values of Different Diseases		
Disease	Transmission	R_0
Ebola	Bodily fluids / ?	1-2
1918 Spanish Flu	Airborne droplet	2-3
SARS	Airborne droplet	2-5
AIDS	Sexual contact	2–5
Mumps	Airborne droplet	4-8
Smallpox	Airborne droplet	5–7
Polio	Fecal-oral route	5–7
Rubella	Airborne droplet	5–7
Measles	Airborne	12–18

Airborne droplets, however, is a different story. Airborne droplets are relatively large (when compared to the dry particles that are suspended in the air by an airborne disease), wet particles, propelled through the air by way of coughing, sneezing or violent vomiting, that land on walls, floors, or other people. It is entirely possible that Ebola is spread via airborne droplets. The CDC still denies this. The WHO downplays the probability. Other experts, especially those who are independent of governmental organizations, are not as quick to dismiss this.

Despite CDC claims that droplet transmission is not possible, it has been shown that VHFs have an infectious dose of 1 to 10 organisms by airborne droplets in non-human primates.

1. Source: Franz, D. R., Jahrling, P. B., Friedlander, A. M., McClain, D. J., Hoover, D. L., Bryne, W. R., Pavlin, J. A., Christopher, G. W., & Eitzen, E. M. (1997). Clinical recognition and management of patients exposed to biological warfare agents. Jama, 278(5), 399-411.)

Additionally, laboratories have been able to demonstrate that primates exposed to airborne droplets from pigs have become infected.

1. Source: Twenhafel, N. A., Mattix, M. E., Johnson, J. C., Robinson, C. G., Pratt, W. D., Cashman, K. A., Wahl-Jensen, V., Terry, C., Olinger, G. G., Hensley, L. E., & Honko, A. N. (2012). Pathology of experimental aerosol Zaire ebolavirus infection in rhesus macaques. Veterinary Pathology Online, 0300985812469636.

2. Source: Mwanatambwe, M., Yamada, N., Arai, S., Shimizu-Suganuma, M., Shichinohe, K., & Asano, G. (2001). Ebola hemorrhagic fever (EHF): mechanism of transmission and pathogenicity. Journal of Nippon Medical School.68 (5), 370-375.

3. Source: Plague. (2004). In R. G. Darling, & J. B. Woods (Eds.), USAMRIID's Medical Management of Biological Casualties Handbook (5th ed., pp. 40-44). Fort Detrick M.D.: USAMRIID.

4. Source: Reed, D. S., Lackemeyer, M. G., Garza, N. L., Sullivan, L. J., & Nichols, D. K. (2011). Aerosol exposure to Zaire ebolavirus in three nonhuman primate species: differences in disease course and clinical pathology. Microbes and Infection, 13(11), 930-936.

5. Source: Feigin, R. D. (Ed.). (2004). Textbook of Pediatric Infectious Diseases (5th Ed.). Philadelphia, USA: Elsevier, Inc.

- Aerosol Transmissibles (Not Confirmed by Authorities): According to The Center for Infectious Disease Research and Policy (CIDRAP), "We believe there is scientific and epidemiologic evidence that Ebola virus has the potential to be transmitted via infectious aerosol particles both near and at a distance from infected patients, which means that healthcare workers should be wearing respirators, not facemasks." They continue, "Modern research, using more sensitive instruments and analytic methods, has shown that aerosols emitted from the respiratory tract contain a wide distribution of particle sizes—including many that are small enough to be inhaled. Thus, both small and large particles will be present near an infectious person.

The chance of large droplets reaching the facial mucous membranes is quite small, as the nasal openings are small and shielded by their external and internal structure. Although close contact may permit large-droplet exposure, it also maximizes the possibility of aerosol inhalation. As noted by early aerobiologists, liquid in a spray aerosol, such as that generated during coughing or sneezing, will quickly evaporate, which increases the concentration of small particles in the aerosol. Because evaporation occurs in milliseconds, many of these particles are likely to be found near the infectious person. The current paradigm also assumes that only "small" particles (less than 5 micrometers [mcm]) can be inhaled and deposited in the respiratory tract. This is not true. Particles as large as 100 mcm (and perhaps even larger) can be inhaled into the mouth and nose. Larger particles are deposited in the nasal passages, pharynx, and upper regions of the lungs, while smaller particles are more likely to deposit in the lower, alveolar regions. And for many pathogens, infection is possible regardless of the particle size or deposition site."

CIDRAP concludes:

"To summarize, for the following reasons we believe that Ebola could be an opportunistic aerosol-transmissible disease requiring adequate respiratory protection:

- o Patients and procedures generate aerosols, and Ebola virus remains viable in aerosols for up to 90 minutes.

- o All sizes of aerosol particles are easily inhaled both near to and far from the patient.

- o Crowding, limited air exchange, and close interactions with patients all contribute to the probability that healthcare workers will be exposed to high concentrations of very toxic infectious aerosols.

- o Ebola targets immune response cells found in all epithelial tissues, including in the respiratory and gastrointestinal system.

- o Experimental data support aerosols as a mode of disease transmission in non-human primates."

The author tends towards CIDRAP's stance. Infection through Direct Contact is certain, and airborne droplet seems likely, but aerosol transmissibles for up to 90 minutes appears possible as well.

The complete CIDRAP article (with multiple sourced studies) can be found here:

http://www.cidrap.umn.edu/news-perspective/2014/09/commentary-health-workers-need-optimal-respiratory-protection-ebola

- Viral Shedding (Not Confirmed by Authorities): Researchers have also observed viral shedding from infected pigs via nasopharyngeal (upper portion of the pharynx, from the base of the skull to the roof of the mouth) secretions and rectal swabs.

1. Source: Kobinger, G. P., Leung, A., Neufeld, J., Richardson, J. S., Falzarano, D., Smith, G., Tierney, K., Patel, A., & Weingartl, H. M. (2011). Replication, pathogenicity, shedding, and transmission of Zaire ebolavirus in pigs. Journal of Infectious Diseases, jir077.

2. Source: Marsh, G. A., Haining, J., Robinson, R., Foord, A., Yamada, M., Barr, J. A., Payne, J., White, J., Yu, M., Bingham, J., Rollin, P. E., Nichol, S. T., Wang, L-F., & Middleton, D. (2011). Ebola Reston virus infection of pigs: clinical significance and transmission potential. Journal of Infectious Diseases, 204(suppl 3), S804-S809.

The author would contend that there are no studies that suggest airborne droplet, aerosolized transmissions and viral shedding in humans is possible because researchers are having a difficult time finding volunteers, with there not being a cure and all.

- Semen: Another means of transmission worth discussing is semen. Studies have suggested that the Ebola Virus may remain transmissible through a survivor's semen for 70 to over 90 days. Survivors should abstain from sexual contact for at least four months, or until additional research can be performed to determine a more precise period of possible infection.

Ebola continues to be present for many weeks after resolution (months in semen). The virus has been identified in breast milk 7 to 15 days after disease onset.

1. Source: Bausch et al. Assessment of the risk of Ebola virus transmission from bodily fluids and fomites. Journal of Infectious Diseases 2007;196:S142-7.

People who recover develop antibodies that may last for at least 10 years. These antibodies may be critical in the development of a viable treatment for the virus.

There is no evidence that mosquitos or other insects can transmit Ebola. Only mammals have displayed the ability to become infected and spread the virus.

When Does an Infected Person Become Contagious?

Authorities say that a person is only contagious once symptoms are present. This may very well be true. The author believes it is also possible that this strain of Ebola may be contagious before symptoms are present. This is merely conjecture, but may also explain how this outbreak has managed to last far longer than any previous outbreaks. The following is a list of other diseases and when an infected person first becomes contagious:

- Chickenpox: One to two days before a rash appears.
- Common Cold: One to two days before symptoms appear.
- Flu (Influenza): Typically one day before symptoms appear.
- Measles: Not definitively established. Measles is most infectious after the first symptoms appear and before the rash develops.
- Mumps: Approximately six days before swelling of the glands.
- Rubella (German measles): One week before a rash appears.
- Shingles: Infectious from when a rash first appears until the last blister has scabbed over. Typically five and seven days after symptoms start.

Based on the above, many diseases are infectious prior to the onset of symptoms. Furthermore, the period from which measles becomes contagious has not been definitively established. Measles was first isolated in 1954 and has been researched much more extensively than Ebola. How then, are authorities uncertain of measles, yet certain of Ebola?

The author contends that there remains a possibility that Ebola may be contagious prior to the onset of symptoms, especially since it has been shown that VHFs have an infectious dose of 1 to 10 organisms by airborne droplets in non-human primates. The author contends that if a small amount of the virus is present in an infected person's bodily fluids, then they are potentially contagious.

Diagnosis

Diagnosing Ebola can be difficult. Early symptoms are common to many different infections. This period of uncertainty allows an infected person to continue on with their lives, possibly infecting others. In Africa, malaria and typhoid fever exhibit the same symptoms, and are far more common. In the West, early symptoms are similar to the flu.

If someone has the early symptoms of Ebola and has had known contact with an infected individual, or infected areas, they should seek medical assistance immediately. Self-isolation should be practiced until authorities can properly quarantine the person. Samples from the person can then be collected and tests can be performed to confirm infection.

Ebola diagnosis tests include:

- Complete Blood Count (CBC)
- Tests to show whether virus-specific antibodies exist in the patient (ELISA)
- Liver function tests
- Coagulation studies (how well the blood clots)

Currently, no rapid means of diagnosing Ebola exists, though methods are in development.

Treatment

Currently, there is no cure for Ebola. Several experimental treatments and vaccines for the disease are under development, but they have not yet been fully vetted. Their effectiveness and safety is yet to be determined.

Currently, treatment is mostly supportive in nature. Management of pain, maintaining oxygen status and blood pressure, providing intravenous (IV) fluids, electrolytes and nutrition can provide some level of comfort and improve the chances of patient survival.

Surviving Ebola is affected by the level of care provided to the patient, as well as their immune system's response to the disease. An immunocompromised person will have greater difficulty surviving the virus, compared to a healthy individual. Survivors of previous outbreaks have been known to develop vision and joint problems, as well as other long-term complications.

The experimental treatments and vaccines currently being considered for use are as follows:

- Brincidofovir (Treatment): An antiviral drug granted emergency FDA approval for investigative treatment, after being found effective against the virus in in-vitro testing. Brincidofovir was administered to treat Thomas Duncan in Dallas.

- <u>BCX4430 (Treatment)</u>: An antiviral drug currently being researched by the U.S. Army Medical Research Institute of Infectious Diseases (USAMRIID).

- <u>Favipiravir (Avigan) (Treatment)</u>: Approved in Japan for stockpiling against influenza pandemics. The drug shows promise based on animal testing. A clinical trial is being planned for patients in Guinea in November 2014. The French Health ministry has authorized its use.

- <u>TKM-Ebola (Treatment)</u>: An RNA interference drug. TKM-Ebola started its Phase 1 trial in early 2014. It has received limited approval from the FDA for emergency use.

- <u>ZMapp (Treatment)</u>: A combination of monoclonal antibodies. The drug has been used to treat seven infected individuals infected with the Ebola virus. Some of them have recovered, but the outcome is not considered to be statistically significant. ZMapp has proven highly effective in a trial involving macaques. October 8, 2014, Texas A&M said it was ready to mass-produce the drug, pending final approval.

- <u>cAd3-ZEBOV (Vaccine)</u>: Currently in Phase 1 trials. GlaxoSmithKline, a joint developer, is stockpiling 10,000 doses in anticipation of its successful completion.

- rVSV-ZEBOV (Vaccine): Pending Phase 1 trials. Developed by the Public Health Agency of Canada. Mass production is not expected until sometime in 2015.

- The WHO has stated that transfusion of whole blood or purified serum from Ebola survivors is the therapy with the greatest potential to be implemented immediately. This method is currently being studied.

Hospitals are not typically designed to isolate and treat BSL-4 diseases. Though they can receive and treat these patients if necessary, the results may be similar to recent events at Texas Presbyterian Hospital; which is, not desirable.

For a hospital to be able to properly treat infected individuals with minimal risk to healthcare workers, it would require a setup such as a separate, secured unit with a self-contained, negative-pressure airflow system. The following facilities have comparable systems:

- Nebraska Medical Center Biocontainment Unit. Omaha, NE. 10 beds. Click on their brochure for information on the capabilities of such a facility.

- St. Patricks Hospital. ICU Isolation Unit. Missoula, MT. Three beds.

- Emory University. Serious Communicable Disease Unit. Atlanta, GA. Three beds.

- National Institute of Health (NIH). Special Clinical Studies Unit. Bethesda, MD. Seven beds.

  In total, the United States has 23 beds in four units capable of properly receiving, isolating and treating Ebola patients.

Chapter 3: The History of Ebola

Chapter 3 is divided into the following sections:

History

The Reston Outbreak

The Numbers

History

The first know outbreak of Ebola occurred in 1976 in Nzara, Sudan. This outbreak infected 284 and killed 151. Patient zero was a storekeeper in a cotton factory. He became symptomatic on June 27, was hospitalized on June 30, and ultimately died on July 6. At this time, the disease was unknown.

In September 1976, a separate outbreak emerged. From it, a specimen arrived at the desk of Peter Piot. Piot was a young scientist at the Institute of Tropical Medicine in Belgium. The specimen was from a colleague stationed in what was then Zaire, now known as the Democratic Republic of the Congo.

A note explained that the sample was taken from a Belgian nun working in a small village deep in the heart of the Congo. She had mysteriously fallen ill and died soon thereafter. And the disease was spreading. Piot's colleague requested the specimen be evaluated immediately so that the disease could be identified and a plan could be formulated.

The crook-shaped organism he saw under the microscope would lead Piot on a journey half way around the world. Two weeks later, the 27-year-old was on a flight to Kinshasa. From there, he and several others would board a C-130 and fly to Bumba, over 500 miles to the north. As soon as they had stepped off the plane, it was in the air again. Fear hung thick in the jungle, the same one that held the origins of the AIDS virus. 75 miles later, over harsh country and dangerous crossings, they arrived in Yambuku, home to an old Spanish Mission. It was ground zero for the mysterious virus that killed indiscriminately.

It was a murder mystery set deep in a rain forest. For three months, the team worked feverishly. Eventually, they began to unravel clues to the virus.

Through quarantines and education, they fought back. Even still, nearly 300 people died. They named it after an obscure tributary that winds its way over 150 miles to the Congo. *Ebola*.

From 1976 to 2012, there have been nearly 2,400 cases and 1,600 deaths from the disease.

The Reston Outbreak

Though many believe we have never had an Ebola outbreak in the United States, this is not necessarily true. The virus, named after Reston, Virginia where it was first discovered, experienced an outbreak at Hazelton Laboratories in 1990. Located within the D.C. metropolitan area, Reston is at the foot of our nation's capital. Richard Preston's 1995 book, The Hot Zone, dramatized the outbreak with terrifying success.

While investigating an outbreak of Simian hemorrhagic fever in November 1989, Thomas Geisbert discovered viruses similar in appearance to Ebola in tissue samples taken from Crab-eating Macaques imported from the Philippines to Hazleton Laboratories. The monkeys' name is derived from the fact that they can often be seen foraging the beaches of Southeast Asia. Over a span of three months, more than a third of the monkeys died at a rate of two to three a day.

Blood samples were taken from the animal handlers during the incident. Of the nearly 180 people, six tested positive using the ELISA method. Nonetheless, they remained asymptomatic. In January 1990, an animal handler at the lab cut himself while dissecting the liver of an infected macaque. The CDC placed him under surveillance, but he also remained asymptomatic. The CDC concluded that this particular strain of the Ebola Virus had a low potential to cause disease in humans.

Hazelton abandoned the lab that same year. In 1995, the facility was demolished. As of 2009, the site housed a daycare. Little remains of the Reston outbreak save for the memories of those that worked there. Had the Reston strain had a slightly different molecular makeup, perhaps we all would know its story, and have the scars to show for it.

The Reston Virus appeared again in Italy in 1992. In 1996, it reemerged at an export facility in the Philippines. A second American outbreak occurred in Texas later that year. The animals were from the same Philippine supplier as the original outbreak in Virginia.

In 2008, pigs in Manila tested positive for it. In 2009, Philippine health officials announced that a hog farm worker had been infected with the virus. The man remained asymptomatic.

Reston is the only known strain of Ebola that did not originate in Africa.

The Numbers

The following table lists all known Ebola outbreaks since 1976, the number of infected cases, and the number of fatalities. Fatality rates have been as low as 25% (With the exception of Cote d'Ivoire in 1994), but typically range from 50%-90%. Overall, the average rate of death is nearly 70%. In the table, DRC refers to the Democratic Republic of the Congo.

Ebola Outbreaks, 1976 - 2012				
Year	Country	Cases	Deaths	Fatality Rate
1976	Sudan	284	151	53%
1976	DRC	318	280	88%
1977	DRC	1	1	100%
1979	Sudan	34	22	65%
1994	Cote d'Ivoire	1	0	0%
1994	Gabon	52	31	60%
1995	DRC	315	254	81%
1996	South Africa	1	1	100%
1996	Gabon	60	45	75%
1996	Gabon	31	21	68%
2000	Uganda	425	224	53%
2001-2002	Congo	59	44	75%
2001-2002	Gabon	65	53	82%
2003	Congo	35	29	83%
2003	Congo	143	128	90%
2004	Sudan	17	7	41%
2005	Congo	12	10	83%
2007	Uganda	149	37	25%
2007	DRC	264	187	71%
2008	DRC	32	14	44%
2011	Uganda	1	1	100%
2012	DRC	57	29	51%
2012	Uganda	7	4	57%
2012	Uganda	24	17	71%
		2387	1590	67%

Historically, outbreaks have been small. A village becomes infected, but since Ebola kills its victims so quickly, the disease burns out before it can spread far. Prior to 2014, the largest outbreak was in Uganda in 2000. 425 people were infected and 224 died.

The following chart provides a visual comparison of the outbreaks.

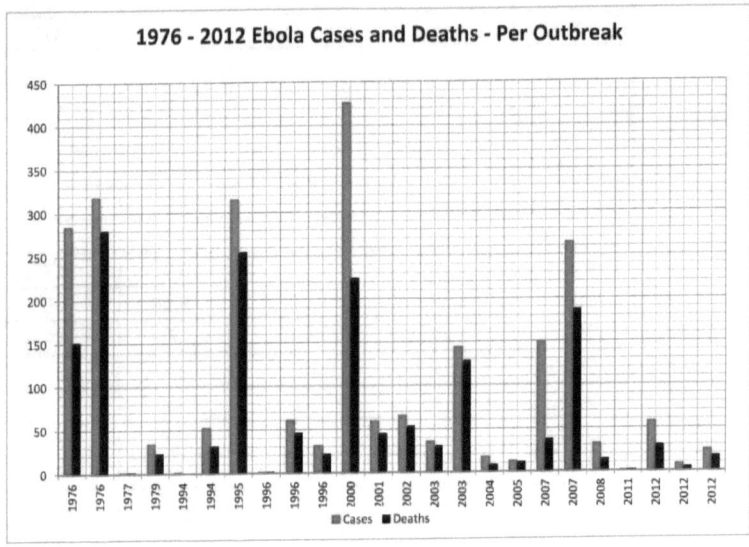

The following map displays the locations of the outbreaks across Africa, as well as the habitat of the fruit bat. The fruit bat is believed to be a natural reservoir for the virus. A natural reservoir allows the virus to survive between outbreaks in humans.

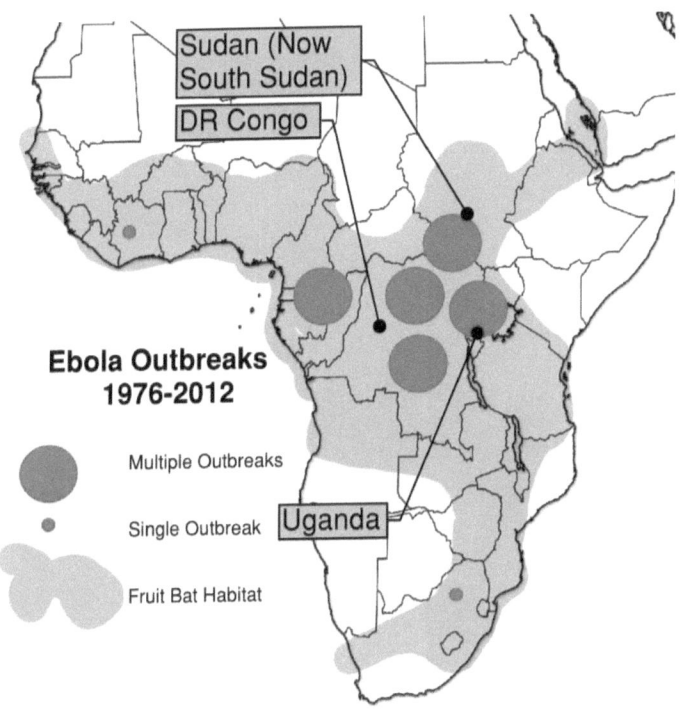

As can be seen, the majority of cases have been in Central Africa. This area is sometimes referred to as the Ebola Belt. Until 2014, no outbreaks had occurred in the western limits of the fruit bat's habitat.

Alex Smith

Chapter 4: The 2014 West African Ebola Outbreak

Chapter 4 is divided into the following sections:

Notes

Guinea

Liberia

Sierra Leone

Other African Countries

Europe

The United States

The Numbers

Notes

If you read this account of the 2014 outbreak on the day this book is published, it will already be outdated. This is still a very dynamic event, and shows no signs of slowing yet. Use the information below as a primer of its beginnings.

A note about case and death numbers reported in this book for the 2014 outbreak:

Numbers include Suspected, Probable and Confirmed cases.

- Suspected: A person who has (or had) sudden onset of high fever and had contact with a suspected, probable or confirmed Ebola case, or a person with sudden onset of high fever and at least three symptoms of Ebola.

- Probable: A person evaluated by a clinician or any person who died from suspected Ebola, and had a link to a confirmed case, but was not confirmed by a lab test.

- Confirmed: A person whose infection was confirmed by a lab test.

Upon initial review, this may lead some to argue that cases and deaths herein are being overstated. However, not all cases can be confirmed. The manpower simply does not exist. Furthermore, in hot zones especially, many contract and die from the virus without ever being reported. Experts concede that actual case and death numbers may be two to three times higher than reported numbers (the numbers the author uses herein). The author contends it could be even higher than that. As you read these numbers, keep this in mind.

Guinea

In December of 2013, a two-year-old boy in Meliandou, Guinea became ill with the virus. He is believed to be the index case, or patient zero. Symptoms began on December 2. He died four days later. On the 13th, his mother passed away. On Christmas day, his sister began to show symptoms of Ebola. By the 29th, she had died as well.

Family members traveled from other villages to attend the funeral of his grandmother, who had also died. They became infected and carried the disease back with them.

A nurse and the village midwife were also infected by the initial victims. In early February, they both died. Through the midwife, the infection was able to spread to another village.

The disease continued to meander through rural Guinea. It moved slowly at first, but gained momentum with every new victim. Soon villages became cities; and cities, entire districts. By March 2014, it was spreading like a wildfire.   The following charts shows the early progression through Guinea:

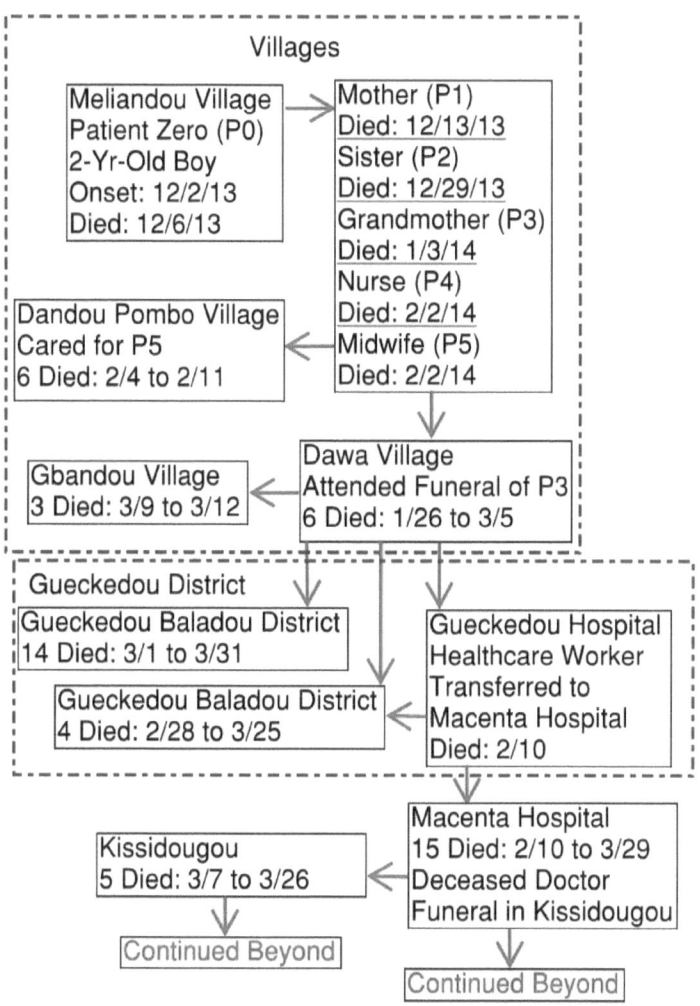

In the early days of the outbreak, there were no rapid-response teams rushed to the hot zone. No coalition of governments converged to provide relief. The main caretakers during the early days were <u>Doctors Without Borders</u> (Médecins Sans Frontières), an international medical and humanitarian foundation, and <u>Samaritan's Purse</u>, an evangelical-Christian humanitarian organization. Neither of these groups were in Africa to combat Ebola. Both were involved in other endeavors. But as the disease spread, they quickly pivoted their attention to the victims in critical need of help. Many of the survivors have these two groups to thank.

On March 31, Ebola had infected 122 people in Guinea and killed 80. It had also begun to spill over into Liberia. The CDC, believing the outbreak to be similar to those in the past, sent a five-person team to assist Guinea's Ministry of Health and the WHO. The group was overwhelmed the moment their plane touched down on the tarmac.

In September, a healthcare team was attacked in a village. Eight people were murdered. Among the dead were three journalists and four volunteers. They were found stuffed in a septic tank. Many Africans do not believe that Ebola exists and are suspicious of outsiders and healthcare workers. Others believe it was created by their government. Still others think that it can only be treated by traditional healers and medicine men. These superstitions only serve to further the spread of the virus. By the end of September, Guinea had over 1,100 cases and over 700 deaths.

Liberia

In late March, by the time the CDC had sent a small team to evaluate the virus and provide oversight to Guinea's Ministry of Health, Ebola had already leaped across the border into Liberia.

By June, the disease had spread to Monrovia, the capital of Liberia and a squalid city of nearly one million people. A pair of bloody civil wars ravaged the country from 1989-2003, with only a three year reprieve in between. Monrovia still bears the scars from that brutal time. The city is crowded beyond imagination. Heaps of garbage line the streets, festering vermin and disease. To say that sanitation is lacking is an incredible understatement. In the coming months, deaths from Ebola would explode as the virus tightened its grip on the city.

In early July, there had been 115 cases and 75 deaths in the country, including the head surgeon at Redemption Hospital just west of the city. The hospital was immediately shut down and its patients were distributed to nearby facilities. It has since reopened, but has repeatedly faced worker strikes and supply shortages.

In August, the country's president had declared a national state of emergency. Rights were suspended. The military was sent into the hot zone to quarantine villages. But the Liberian military is rife with corruption. Soldiers reportedly took bribes and allowed villagers to leave. The attempt to contain the spread of the virus had failed. The end of the month marked a staggering 1,700 cases and over 870 deaths.

By mid-September, 1,700 cases had mushroomed to over 2,700. Of those, over 1,400 had died. Ebola had found a country that was ripe for the taking. Hospitals were abandoned. Those that still stood could hardly be considered functional. Medical supplies were all but nonexistent.

In October 2014, officials admitted the nation was beginning to crumble. Senatorial elections were cancelled for fear that the ballot box would further spread the disease. As of October 8, there had been 4,076 cases and 2,316 deaths in Liberia alone.

Liberia is at particular risk for continued spread of the virus. There are only approximately 50 doctors in the entire country. That translates to about one doctor for every 81,850 citizens (1:81,850).

Sierra Leone

Sierra Leone is the third nation to be affected by the current outbreak. In April, Gambia banned flights from the country, even though the government denied any cases existed.

In May 2014, a medicine woman that had been treating an infected patient fell ill and died. By the end of the month, 50 cases and 6 deaths had been reported.

In June, a state of emergency was declared in the Kailahun District, which borders Liberia and Guinea. Checkpoints were erected. Schools were closed. Seasonal flooding also began, which hampered efforts to combat the spread of the virus. 239 cases and 99 deaths were reported by month's end.

In July, Sierra Leone's only VHF expert died after contracting Ebola in his clinic. 574 cases and 252 deaths were reported.

In August, the nation's health minister was removed from office. Radio and loudspeaker awareness campaigns were enacted in Freetown, a crowded city of 1.2 million people and the capital of Sierra Leone. The country also passed a law that criminalized hiding from authorities while infected with the virus. Anyone caught would face two years in jail, if they survived the disease. By the end of the month, 1,216 cases and 436 deaths were reported.

In September, the nation imposed a three-day lockdown on its population. From the 19th to the 21st, over 2,800 workers and volunteers went door-to-door to provide education on how to prevent infection. Community surveillance teams were also established. 80% of the targeted households were reached in the three days and approximately 150 new cases were discovered. By the end of the month, five districts were under isolation. Only essential services and deliveries were to be allowed passage. Despite these efforts, the disease entered a state of exponential growth. Cases began to double every 20 to 30 days. September to October is also "malaria season", adding further load to the already collapsing healthcare system. Cases had swelled to 2,317. Deaths were reported at 570.

By October, hospitals were exhausting all medical supplies. Burial crews began striking. 36,000 people were quarantined. Reportedly, unburied corpses can be seen in piles in the city. Meanwhile, victims of other diseases are dying at higher than normal rates, since Ebola has taken precedence. On October 8, 2,950 cases and 930 deaths had been reported. Officials concede that these numbers are gross understatements.

Other African Countries

Nigeria

On July 20, 2014, a Liberian-American flew into Lagos, Nigeria. The city is the nation's capital and home to a staggering 17.5 to 21 million people. By the time his plane touched down, he was violently ill. He was immediately taken to the hospital and isolated. He died five days later. The victim's contacts were quickly identified and monitored for signs of infection.

On August 19, the doctor that treated Nigeria's index case died. The doctor was lauded as a hero for quickly isolating his patient and refusing his release. By September, Nigeria claimed to be free of Ebola. On October 20, if no new cases are noted, the WHO will confirm this declaration. As of October 8, there have been 20 cases and 8 deaths in the country.

Senegal

On August 29, 2014, a university student from Guinea was being treated for Ebola in Dakar, Senegal. He has since recovered. No new cases have been reported.

Europe

Several European countries have flown citizens infected in Africa home for treatment.

Spain is the only European country in which an infection has occurred on their soil. In October 2014, a nurse who had cared for victims that had been medically evacuated from Africa to Spain had fallen ill. Her dog, Excalibur was euthanized to prevent a carrier risk. This resulted in violent clashes between police and protesters.

The United States

- On September 20, 2014, Thomas Duncan arrived in Dallas, Texas. He had flown from Monrovia, where he had come into contact with an Ebola victim. It is not certain if he was aware the victim was infected.

- On September 24, Duncan began to experience symptoms of Ebola.

- On September 25, Duncan went to the Texas Health Presbyterian Hospital emergency room. The ER nurse recorded his travel history. He was prescribed antibiotics and discharged.

- On September 28, Duncan began to vomit violently, and was transported to the hospital by ambulance.

- On September 30, 2014, Duncan became the first Ebola victim in the United States diagnosed with Ebola.

- On October 1, Duncan's contacts began to be monitored.

- By October 4, his condition had deteriorated to critical. Doctors began administering the experimental drug Brincidofovir. Stocks of ZMapp, which had been used successfully on previous patients, had been depleted.

- On October 8, Duncan died. Following his death,

screening procedures were enacted at several airports. Multiple reports of breaches in screening protocol have been reported. There is also much criticism regarding the current screening system's effectiveness even when performed properly.

- On October 10, a nurse at the same hospital began to exhibit symptoms.

- On October 11, she tested positive for Ebola. She was wearing full PPE. Though the CDC states safety protocol was breached, the nurse has said she is not aware of having broken any protocol. The hospital reiterated her claims.

- Authorities have decided not to immediately euthanize her dog, despite the risk that it may become a carrier of the disease.

- Although numerous African and European countries have banned flights from Guinea, Liberia and Sierra Leone, the United States has thus far refused to do so.

- On October 7, the U.S. SOUTHCOM commander warned that the, "nightmare scenario is right around the corner." He added, "Of the homeland security folks doing their work on our southwest border, of the number of people they capture, a very large percentage of them are West Africans." He also stated that, "If Ebola breaks out in Haiti or in Central America, I think it's literally 'Katie bar the door' in terms of the mass migration of Central Americans into the United States." He later added, "So these populations will move to either run away from Ebola or in the fear of having been infected to get to the United States where they will be taken care of."

The Numbers

The following tables recount the cases and deaths that have been discussed in the sections above.

Date	Guinea Cases	Guinea Deaths	Liberia Cases	Liberia Deaths	Sierra Leone Cases	Sierra Leone Deaths	Total Cases	Total Deaths
3/22	49	29					49	29
3/24	86	59					86	59
3/25	86	60					86	60
3/26	86	62					86	62
3/27	103	66					103	66
3/28	112	70					112	70
3/29	112	70	2	1			114	71
3/31	122	80	8	2			130	82
4/1	127	83	8	5			135	88
4/7	151	95	21	10			172	105
4/9	158	101	21	10			179	111
4/10	158	101	25	11			183	112
4/11	158	101	26	11			184	112
4/14	168	108	26	11			194	119
4/16	197	122	27	11			224	133
4/17	203	129	27	11			230	140
4/20	208	136	27	11			235	147
4/21	208	136	33	11			241	147
4/23	218	141	33	11			251	152
4/24	218	141	33	11			251	152
4/30	221	146	33	11			254	157
5/1	226	149	33	11			259	160
5/2	226	149	33	11			259	160
5/3	231	155	33	11			264	166
5/7	236	158	33	11			269	169
5/10	233	157	33	11			266	168
5/12	248	171	33	11			281	182
5/18	253	176	33	11			286	187
5/23	258	174	33	11			291	185
5/27	281	186	33	11	16	5	330	202
5/28	291	193	33	11	16	5	340	209
5/29	291	193	33	11	50	6	374	210
6/1	328	208	33	11	79	6	440	225
6/3	344	215	33	11	79	6	456	232
6/5	351	226	33	11	81	6	465	243
6/6	351	226	33	11	89	7	473	244

	Guinea		Liberia		Sierra Leone		Total	
Date	Cases	Deaths	Cases	Deaths	Cases	Deaths	Cases	Deaths
6/10	372	236	33	11	89	7	494	254
6/15	394	263	33	24	95	46	522	333
6/16	398	264	33	24	95	46	526	334
6/17	398	264	33	24	97	49	528	337
6/20	390	270	33	24	158	34	581	328
6/22	390	270	51	34	158	34	599	338
6/30	413	303	107	65	239	99	759	467
7/2	412	305	115	75	252	101	779	481
7/6	408	307	131	84	305	127	844	518
7/8	409	309	142	88	337	142	888	539
7/12	406	304	172	105	386	194	964	603
7/14	411	310	174	106	397	197	982	613
7/17	410	310	196	116	442	206	1,048	632
7/20	415	314	224	127	454	219	1,093	660
7/23	427	319	249	129	525	224	1,201	672
7/27	460	339	329	156	533	233	1,322	728
7/30	472	346	391	227	574	252	1,437	825
8/1	485	358	468	255	646	273	1,599	886
8/4	495	363	516	282	691	286	1,702	931
8/6	495	367	554	294	717	298	1,766	959
8/9	506	373	599	323	730	315	1,835	1,011
8/11	510	377	670	355	783	334	1,963	1,066
8/13	519	380	786	413	810	348	2,115	1,141
8/16	543	394	834	466	848	365	2,225	1,225
8/18	579	396	972	576	907	374	2,458	1,346
8/20	607	406	1,082	624	910	392	2,599	1,422
8/25	648	430	1,378	694	1,026	422	3,052	1,546
8/31	771	494	1,698	871	1,216	436	3,685	1,801
9/3	823	522	1,863	1,078	1,292	452	3,978	2,052
9/7	861	557	2,081	1,137	1,424	476	4,366	2,170
9/10	899	568	2,415	1,307	1,509	493	4,823	2,368
9/14	942	601	2,720	1,461	1,655	516	5,317	2,578
9/17	965	623	3,022	1,578	1,753	537	5,740	2,738
9/21	1,022	635	3,280	1,707	1,940	550	6,242	2,892
9/23	1,074	648	3,458	1,830	2,021	557	6,553	3,035
9/25	1,103	668	3,564	1,922	2,120	561	6,787	3,151
9/28	1,157	710	3,696	1,998	2,317	570	7,170	3,278
10/1	1,199	739	3,834	2,069	2,437	623	7,470	3,431
10/5	1,298	768	3,924	2,210	2,789	879	8,011	3,857
10/8	1,350	778	4,076	2,316	2,950	930	8,376	4,024
Note: Other Countries Omitted For Clarity Purposes								

Large increases in cases and deaths typically align with the time periods in which the virus spread into large population centers, such as Monrovia and Freetown. The following graph provides a visual representation of the cases and deaths, and begins to show the markings of exponential progression.

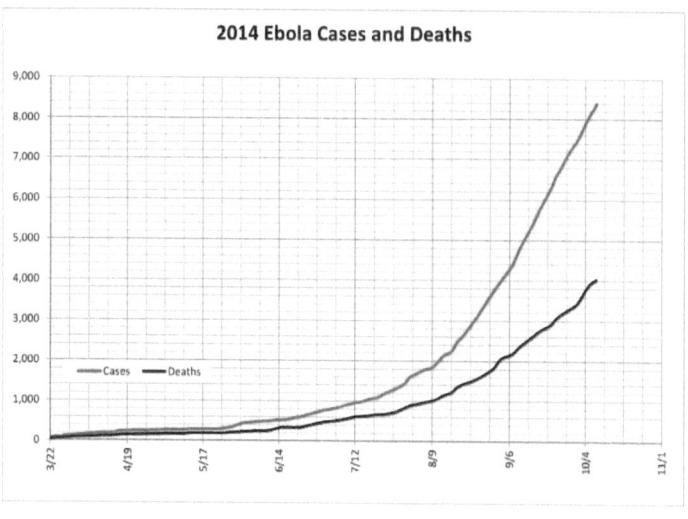

It should be noted that cases and deaths on a certain date should not be compared for the purpose of determining the death rate. This is often done, and may be excused as a simplistic means of comparison. For instance, as of October 8, there have been 8,399 cases and 4,033 deaths. This would appear to result in a death rate of 48%. However, we are not certain if the new cases reported on the 8th will live or die. Therefore, the actual death rate of the cases as of the 8th may be much higher than 48%. A more accurate death rate will not be determinable until the end of the outbreak. Even then, a true death rate <u>may never be known</u>, since the affected nations are overwhelmed and underreporting of cases is rampant.

The following is a bar chart comparing historical outbreaks with the current outbreak.

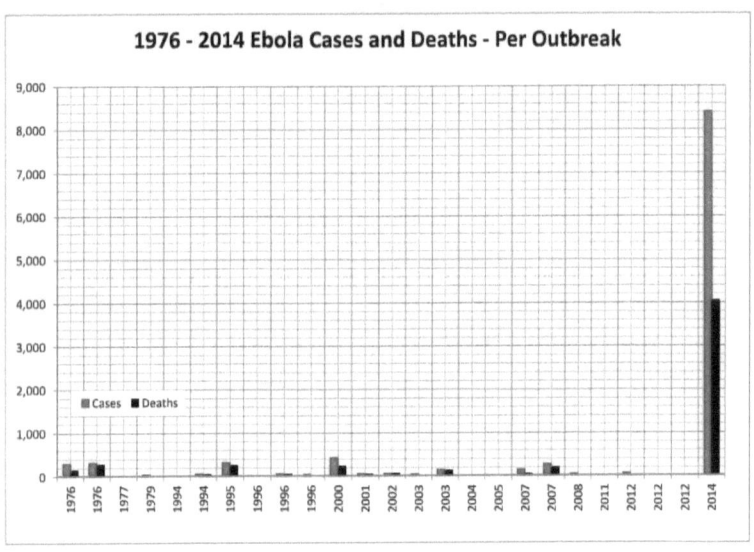

As can be seen, no previous outbreaks come remotely close to the current devastation. Ebola Virus cases have been doubling approximately every month since June.

Note: The 2014 outbreak in the Democratic Republic of the Congo is a separate outbreak from West Africa. As of October 5, 2014, there have been 70 cases and 43 deaths.

Chapter 5: Early Stage – What to do Now

Now that we understand what Ebola is capable of, we must take action now to protect ourselves if the virus continues to spread.

- Have a Plan. Having a plan while a threat is not imminent is critical to your success. During a crisis, when panic abounds, it is better to refer to a plan that was developed while you were able to think objectively. Right now, this is your primary goal. Develop a formal, written plan that can be put into action if a crisis arises. Discuss it with your family. At a minimum, your plan should address:

  o When you quit going to work/school.

  o When you quit leaving your home.

  o How to handle family members that show up at your home that could potentially be infected. Consider quarantining them in a tent or building outside of your home, or perhaps in their vehicle, for several weeks.

- When to flee to a family member's home in an area with fewer/no outbreaks. This should be discussed in detail with everyone involved, *especially* those whom you would be fleeing to. For additional information on this subject, see my book titled: Getting Home.

- How to self-quarantine upon arriving at your destination. Ensure you have sufficient food, water, toiletries, etc. available for your use until you have shown that your are not infected. These may be brought by you are provided upon your arrival.

- Become accustomed to minimizing personal contact. Avoid shaking hands when possible.

- Become accustomed to washing your hands after coming in contact with fomites. From the glossary, fomites are defined as any object that could transfer the disease from one person to another. Doorknobs, cash, ATMs, etc. are all examples. If you cannot immediately wash your hands, use hand sanitizer with at least 70% ethyl alcohol content.

- When possible, avoid areas that could be a focus of infection. These areas include airports, taxis, subways, public gatherings, etc.

- Build a reserve of cash on hand, as well as savings in the bank. In the event of a crisis, you will need both. Aim for three months of savings and cash. Six months is even better.

- Stock a reserve of PPEs such as N99 or N100 masks, rubber boots, rubber gloves, Tyvek coveralls, etc. See Chapter 10 for details.

- Stock appropriate disinfecting agents such as bleach, vinegar and rubbing alcohol. Note that the shelf life of bleach is relatively short. Because of this, having Calcium Hypochlorite (pool shock) on hand to make your own bleach would be prudent. Making bleach from pool shock will be discussed further in Chapter 8.

- Stock food and water for use in the event of a large-scale quarantine. Several months' supply of both would be a desirable goal. See Chapter 10 for additional information.

- Stay abreast of breaking news from both official and (reliable) unofficial sources. Compare both sources and learn to trust your gut if you believe a person in authority is downplaying an event in an attempt to minimize public panic. Do not wait for the masses to panic, have all necessary supplies beforehand.

- Begin discussions with your employer about working from home, if possible. You do not have to mention Ebola in particular, if it would make for an uncomfortable discussion. You could simply say that you are considering the option as a means to reduce transportation costs in your budget.

- Develop alternative sources of income in the event your plan dictates that you should no longer go to work. Bonus points if you are able to earn this income from home, without interacting with others.

- Maintain a healthy diet. Since there is currently very little that can be done medically to combat Ebola, having a strong immune system may be one of the few things you can do to improve your chances of survival if you find yourself infected.

Chapter 6: Advanced Stage – Outbreaks in Your State/Province/Region

If you find that conditions continue to deteriorate, be prepared to institute additional measure, including:

- Minimize excursions from the home. Go to work/school and then immediately home.

- Work from home if possible.

- Use vacation time or sick leave to minimize the amount of time you are at work.

- Consider using rubber gloves when shopping, fueling your vehicle, etc.

  - Learn how to properly remove used gloves so as to avoid exposure.

- Keep hand sanitizer on your person, in your vehicle, etc. at all times. Use religiously.

- Wash your hands after all interactions.

- Moisturize hands to avoid dryness and cracking of the skin, which could result in a higher likelihood of infection.

- Cover all open sores with waterproof dressings.

- Refrain from wearing jewelry.

- Contact all family members that are a part of your <u>written plan</u>. Discuss the state of the outbreak and decide if additional preparations should be made at this time.

- Consider executing the relocation portion of your plan. If you are trying to decide which family member's home is the most suitable for relocation to, consider my book <u>Staying Home</u>.

- Be mindful of the reactions of the people in your community. Panic can spread rapidly through a population and can lead to increased criminal activity and social unrest. Avoid areas that are most susceptible to this.

- Monitor how people react to hot zones similar to your area. Does hospital staff or first responders go on strike? Is the grid (water, power, communications, etc.) affected? Is looting occurring? Is the Just-in-Time (JIT) delivery system failing? Assume what happens elsewhere may happen again if an outbreak occurs in your area. Adjust your plan accordingly.

- Monitor hot zones for what they did right and what mistakes they made. Adjust your plan accordingly.

- Note if local/regional economies are failing in hot zones.

- Remember TDD:

  o Time: Epidemics stop when new infections stop.

  o Distance: If possible, stay at least 10' away from anywhere an infected person has been or anything they might have touched.

  o Disinfection: Heat, UV or oxidation. Discussed more in Chapter 8.

Alex Smith

Chapter 7: Crisis Stage – Epidemic in Your Area

If the virus reaches your immediate area, consider yourself in the midst of a crisis and immediately institute extreme precautions.

- Stay at home. Do not leave for any reason.

- …If you absolutely must leave, wear full PPE and create a decontamination area outside of your home. The area should be outfitted with:

  - Bleach trays to walk through for your shoes.

  - Bleach spray bottles. A spray will require the assistance of another person.

  - Drying racks for bleached items.

  - Decontamination will be discussed in greater detail in Chapters 8 and 9.

- Develop a quarantine area outside of your home in the event that friends or family arrives to stay with you. The area should be sufficiently supplied so that someone could remain in the area for several weeks without requiring interaction with you. The point of the area is to segregate and monitor the new arrivals for symptoms, until it is certain they are not infected.

- You may find yourself in the awkward situation between a regional outbreak and a full-blown epidemic. This may cause you to make the decision to stay at home while normal services are still ongoing. In the event that mail delivery is still functional, retrieve your mail with gloved hands. Microwave the mail for two minutes to ensure it is free of infection. The microwave should not be in the house. Place it in your decontamination area.

- Avoid animals that are potential carriers. This includes both wild animals <u>and</u> pets that may be living outdoors. If a severe outbreak occurs in your immediate area and you have pets living outdoors, you will be faced with a heartbreaking choice: risk infection from your pets, or humanely euthanize them to protect your family. Furthermore, understand that the authorities may decide to euthanize animals to reduce the spread of the disease. Madrid (Spain) health authorities euthanized Excalibur, the dog owned by the first Spanish Ebola patient, Teresa Ramos. This was done in spite of mass protests to save the dog.

- Prepare for potential civil unrest. After Excalibur was euthanized in Spain, protesters clashed with police in the streets. Imagine the response if authorities began mass euthanization of animals, or forced quarantining of people? Do not allow yourself to be a part of any unrest that erupts in your area. Doing so will only increase your risk of infection.

- In the event of mass strikes of healthcare workers, first responders, etc., panic will ensue. Protests and looting may erupt. Economies may crash. Martial law may be instituted. Supplies may dwindle. At this point, YOYO (You're On Your Own). Be able to provide food, water and other basic needs for your family.

- Have the proper training in firearms handling to protect life and property, if need be.

- Remember the following:

    - **Use** precautions with all potentially infected persons.

    - **Identify** suspected cases through symptoms.

    - **Assume** Ebola until proven otherwise.

    - **Isolate** the person until authorities arrive.

    - **Wear** PPEs when necessary.

    - **Disinfect** reusable supplies and equipment immediately after each use.

    - **Dispose** of waste properly and immediately in a burn pit.

    - **Practice** safe burial procedures if authorities are unable to assist with this.

    - **Make** preparations in advance.

Chapter 8: Disinfection

Disinfection Methods

- 3% acetic acid. Commercial vinegar is typically 3% to 5% acetic acid by volume. Check product labels to verify concentrations.

- 1% glutaraldehyde. A solution of 10% W/W glutaraldehyde is sold under the name "Diswart Solution" to remove warts. Note that W/W (weight / weight) is not the same as V/V (volume / volume). If you are not experienced with converting solutions from W/W to V/V, use another disinfection method.

- 70% to 90% ethyl alcohol and alcohol-based products.

- 70% to 90% rubbing alcohol (isopropyl) is acceptable for disinfecting reusable medical instruments. Alcohol should be changed weekly.

- 5.25% household bleach (sodium hypochlorite), and calcium hypochlorite (bleach powder / pool shock) solutions (1:10 to 1:100 for at least 10 minutes). The WHO recommends flooding areas infected by bodily fluids or blood with a 1:10 dilution of 5.25% household bleach for 10 minutes for surfaces that can tolerate it. For surfaces that may corrode or discolor, they recommend careful cleaning to remove visible stains, followed by a 1:100 dilution of 5.25% household bleach for more than 10 minutes. Personally, the author is not worried about discoloration if he is cleaning up Ebola. He will stick with the 1:10 solution. Caution, a 1:10 bleach solution is caustic. If 1:10 is too strong for your use, 1:100 will suffice (or any solution between 1:10 and 1:100 that is tolerable). Avoid inhaling bleach fumes whenever possible.

- Heat. Heat the fomite for 30 to 60 minutes at 60°C (140°F). <u>This method is not advisable</u>, since in a residential setting this would typically require bringing the infected item into a kitchen and placing it in an oven. <u>It goes without saying, do not do this.</u> If no other means were available, disinfection via fire would be an option.

- Boiling. Boil fomites for 5-10 minutes. The author would follow-up with a chemical treatment, such as bleach, to ensure proper disinfection has occurred.

- Any disinfectant that is rated to be effective against non-enveloped viruses. Non-enveloped viruses are harder to kill than enveloped viruses. Ebola is an enveloped virus.

- Waste may be disposed of via incineration. There will be no infectious organisms in the smoke. <u>Even still, avoid inhalation.</u>

Because the effectiveness of diluted bleach decays over time, working solutions should be prepared fresh every 24 hours. Larger outbreaks will require larger quantities of bleach. They should still be made daily. Do not shortcut this measure.

Do not mix bleach with other cleaning agents (such as ammonia). Toxic fumes could be produced.

Paper and cotton are cellulose-based materials. Cellulose reduces the effectiveness of bleach. Higher concentrations of bleach can compensate for this. Do not leave paper towels or cotton cloths in an open cleaning bucket containing diluted bleach.

Making Bleach

The average shelf life of bleach is approximately six months. Afterwards, it will lose around 20% of its strength in the first year and 20% every following year. If you are not rotating bleach stocks, they may not be as concentrated as you expect. This could be deadly in a clean-up scenario. So, how do you store bleach long term?

Calcium Hypochlorite.

Household bleach is Sodium Hypochlorite. You can find Calcium Hypochlorite (pool shock) at your local swimming pool supply store. When stored in a cool, dark place, pool shock has a shelf life of approximately 10 years. It is also very concentrated, allowing you to store more supplies in a smaller area. The following instructions were taken from the Army Technical Bulletin titled, "Sanitary Control & Surveillance of Field Water Supplies" (TB MED 577). The manual can be found here:

http://armypubs.army.mil/med/DR_pubs/dr_a/pdf/tbmed577.pdf

Print and store a copy of this manual for future use.

Steps:

- Select a brand of pool shock that contains <u>at least 70% available chlorine</u>.

- Mix 4 tablespoons of Calcium Hypochlorite to 3 cups of water.

  - 4 tablespoons = 0.25 cups

- If you used a pool shock with 70% available chlorine, this will yield a solution of approximately 5.8% chlorine, or the approximate concentration of standard household bleach.

  - (0.25 cups x 70% / 3 = 0.058 = 5.8%)

- Adjust your formula as needed, based the percentage of available chlorine in the pool shock, and the desired percentage of chlorine in the resulting solution.

Alex Smith

Chapter 9: Establishing Safe Practices

The below items are not to be taken lightly and should not be attempted if the healthcare system is even remotely functional. The below discussion assumes the unthinkable has happened: authorities are unable to contain the virus, the healthcare system has collapsed, and individuals are forced to weather the epidemic on their own (YOYO).

Sections:

Safe Practices

Isolation Room

Changing Room

Quarantine Area

Disinfecting Instruments with Alcohol

Disinfecting Instruments with Bleach

Disinfecting a Bedpan or Waste Bucket

Disinfecting Spills

Disinfecting Walls

Disinfecting PPEs (or Bed Sheets/Sheeting)

Disinfecting Rubber Boots

Disinfecting Mattresses

First Aid for Contaminated Needle or Other Sticking Injury

First Aid for Contact With Body Fluids

Incinerating Waste

Preparing a Body

Safe Practices

- Isolate potentially infected persons at all times. A combination of fever greater than 101°F for longer than 72 hours, rapid weak pulse and unexplained bleeding should be assumed to be Ebola, in the absence of proper tests.

- Even if PPEs are worn, limit the number of healthy individuals that enter an isolation area.

- If possible, only use single-use towels. Sharing, reusing and laundering towels introduces instances to spread the virus.

- Wash the <u>entirety of your hands and forearms</u> with soap and warm water. Be careful not to miss any areas. In short, wash your hands as if you are OCD. This cannot be stated enough.

- Where possible, use disposable items when dealing with infected persons.

- <u>Spills</u>: In the event of a spill of contaminated fluids, allow the aerosols to settle. According to CIDRAP, this could take as long as 90 minutes. While wearing proper PPE, cover the spill with paper towels and apply a disinfectant, such as bleach. Start at the edge and work towards the center. Allow sufficient contact time before clean up.

- <u>Disposal</u>: Decontaminate all materials for disposal by disinfection or incineration. This includes both liquid and solid wastes.

- If a bleach solution no longer smells of bleach, the concentration is no longer strong enough. Replace immediately. Rewash any areas or items cleaned with the diluted or otherwise insufficient solution.

- Use liquid soap in a dispenser rather than bar soap to avoid contamination of the bar. It is preferred that the dispenser is battery operated.

- If liquid soap is unavailable, use cake soap or laundry detergent. Cake soap should be mixed in water to form a sudsy solution. If possible, use an empty liquid clothes detergent bottle with a valve for storing the soapy water. Otherwise, use a ladle to dip the soapy water from a bucket. Disinfect the ladle or valve after every use.

- Do not recap used needles. An accidental sticking could occur.

- Dispose of all sharps in a container that cannot be punctured.

- Routinely clean and disinfect frequently touched surfaces. Again, embrace your OCD.

Isolation Room

- Ideally, an isolation room for infected individuals should be a single room with an adjoining toilet, unconnected to the living area of healthy individuals.

- If the above layout is unavailable, choose a separate building (such as an outbuilding) with no toilet, rather than a room in the living area with a toilet. If necessary, a latrine should be constructed in or alongside the outbuilding. Keeping the infected individuals isolated from healthy individuals is of the utmost importance. This supersedes the need for optimal patient quarters.

- Adequate ventilation is a necessity due to the large amounts of bleach that will be required.

- Access to isolation should be restricted using barriers and signs. Only authorized individuals in full PPE should be allowed entry.

- Rinse gloved hands in a 1:10 bleach solution upon leaving the patient isolation room. If bleach is in short supply, a 1:100 solution will suffice.

- Remove bleach solutions daily, or sooner if the solution becomes cloudy or bloody.

- Anyone handling contaminated items for disinfection purposes or otherwise should wear the same full PPE as those providing direct patient care.

- Items required for the isolation room:

  o Bed (or sleeping mat) for each patient.

  o Plastic sheeting to cover the mattress (or sleeping mat).

  o Bedding.

  o Bedside table.

  o Clock with second hand for measuring pulse and respiration rate.

  o One bedpan per patient.

  o One stethoscope, one thermometer, and one blood-pressure cuff per patient. These should remain in the isolation room with the patient.

  o Covered container for bleach solution used to disinfect thermometer and stethoscope after each use.

  o Barriers around beds, such as screens, hung sheets or curtains, to prevent transmission between patients, if more than one exists.

- o Disinfection station with bleach, soap and water, buckets, sprayer, mop, and single-use towels for cleanups.

- o Wastebaskets.

- o Boot sprayer and pan for disinfecting boots before leaving the room. Disinfecting boots is discussed in detail below.

Changing Room

- The changing room is for care providers. Changing rooms should be completely separated from isolation rooms.

- Contaminated items should be removed from the changing room as soon as possible.

- Items required for the changing room:

  o Hangers for reusable protective clothing.

  o Duct tape for taping cuffs and trousers of protective clothing.

  o Disinfection station with bleach solution for disinfecting gloved hands.

  o Hand washing station with, soap, water, bucket and single-use towels.

  o Wastebaskets.

  o Hampers for reusable PPEs.

Quarantine Area

- The quarantine area is for new arrivals that may or may not be infected.

- Wear full PPE when interacting with new arrivals.

- Inform them they must be quarantined for at least 21 days prior to entering any areas frequented by healthy individuals.

- Area should be a tent, outbuilding or other facility that will provide shelter for the new arrivals. If none of these options exist, arrivals may have to sleep in their vehicle or even in the open.

- Any items provided to new arrivals (water bottles, plates, utensils, hygiene products, etc.) should preferably be disposable. Items should be considered to be contaminated and disposed of as such.

- New arrivals should be monitored daily for symptoms. A detailed record should be kept of all individuals. Temperature, heart rate, breathing, and other vitals should be monitored and recorded.

- If new arrivals become combative regarding the quarantine, they should be asked to leave immediately. Noncompliance places all healthy individuals at risk.

Disinfecting Instruments with Alcohol

- Use 70% to 90% rubbing alcohol.

- Change the alcohol at least once a week.

- Use a single-use towel and dip it in the alcohol.

- Carefully wipe the instrument.

- Hold the towel around it for 30 seconds to one minute.

- Allow instrument to air-dry.

- Discard the towel in a container to be burned.

Disinfecting Instruments with Bleach

- Use a 1:100 bleach solution.

- Change the bleach at least once a day.

- Use a clean single-use towel and dip it in the alcohol.

- Never dip a soiled towel in the bleach.

- Carefully wipe the instrument with the bleached towel.

- Alternatively, soak instrument in a 1:10 bleach solution.

- Allow to soak for 10 minutes.

- Allow instrument to air-dry.

- Discard the towel in a container to be burned.

Disinfecting a Bedpan or Waste Bucket

- Use a 1:10 bleach solution. Cover contents with solution.

- Empty contents directly into toilet.

- Clean bedpan with soap and water to remove any remaining solids.

- Rinse bedpan with 1:100 bleach solution.

Disinfecting Spills

- Pour bleach over spill.

- Use 1:10 if spills are dense. Otherwise, use 1:100.

- Allow to soak for 15 minutes.

- Remove spill solids with a 1:100 bleach solution-soaked towel.

- Discard the towel in a container to be burned.

- Wash area with soap and water.

- Allow to air dry.

Disinfecting Walls

- Spray wall with 1:100 bleach solution.

- Use low pressure and apply close to wall to minimize aerosols and splashing.

- Alternatively, apply with mop.

- Afterwards, wash area with soap and water.

- Allow to air dry.

Disinfecting PPEs (or Bed Sheets/Sheeting)

- Use a designated area for PPE cleaning.

- Place PPEs in bucket containing 1:100 bleach solution.

- Soak for 30 to 45 minutes. Ensure all items are fully submerged.

- Remove PPEs

- Rinse and place in a bucket containing soapy water.

- Soak overnight.

- Scrub to remove stains.

- Allow to air dry, preferably in direct sunlight.

Disinfecting Rubber Boots

- Step into a pan with 2" of 1:100 bleach solution.

- Spray the remainder of boot with 1:100 bleach solution.

- Use low pressure and apply close to boots to minimize aerosols and splashing.

- Change pan daily, or sooner if solution becomes cloudy or bloody.

Disinfecting Mattresses

- Pour 1:10 bleach solution directly onto mattress.

- Allow to completely soak through.

- Wait 30 to 45 minutes.

- Flood with soapy water.

- Wait 5 to 10 minutes.

- Rinse with clean water.

- Allow mattress to dry in sun for several days, rotating as needed.

First Aid for Contaminated Needle or Other Sticking Injury

- Immerse injured area in 70% rubbing alcohol.

- Soak for 30 to 45 seconds.

- Wash affected area with soapy water.

- Flush with running water for 30 to 60 seconds.

- Apply normal first aid, as needed.

First Aid for Contact With Body Fluids

- Flush area with soap and clean water immediately.

- Soak area in 70% rubbing alcohol for 30 to 60 seconds.

- If eyes, flush with running water for 10 to 15 minutes.

- Take full shower.

Incinerating Waste

- Wear full PPE while transporting waste to disposal pit and during burns.

- Discard waste in pit.

- Pit should be approximately 6' deep. Pit should be wide enough to completely contain any items to be disposed in it.

- Douse waste with fuel. Do not use gasoline, due to the risk of burn injury. Use charcoal lighter fluid.

- Light fire from a distance by dropping a burning paper towel or other flammable item into the pit. Item should be clean, not contaminated.

- Ensure items are fully incinerated.

- Once pit is half-full of ashes, cover and dig a new pit.

Preparing a Body

- This should only be undertaken if your healthcare system has completely collapsed. This information is a last resort.

- Contact authorities immediately.

- Evacuate area.

- Wear full PPE when interacting with the body.

- Spray body and the surrounding area with a 1:10 bleach solution.

- Wrap the body in plastic sheeting and secure in a body bag, if available.

- If a body bag is unavailable, seal with duct tape and apply a second layer of plastic sheeting and seal with duct tape.

- Spray bag (or both interior and exterior plastic sheeting) with a 1:10 bleach solution.

- Wait for authorities to arrive and dispose of body.

- If authorities are unable to assist due to a collapsed system, remove body from any areas inhabited by healthy individuals.

- Bury body at least 6' deep.

- Mark location so that it may be exhumed later by authorities.

Alex Smith

Chapter 10: Preparations

What You Need For When You Need it Most

The following is a list of items to help you survive a serious, grid-down disaster. Medical supplies will be discussed first, followed by Other supplies.

Medical

- Boots: Boots or overboots must be worn in lieu of, or over, shoes. Standard rubber boots are acceptable. A minimum height of 12" is required. Soles should be textured. If no boots are available, three layers of plastic bags will suffice. Boots should never be shared.

- Face Shields: Face shields do not take the place of facemasks or respirators. Always wear both. If eye contamination is suspected, rinse eyes immediately with a saline solution or clean water. See previous chapter for details regarding eye contamination.

- Foot/Leg Covers: For protection during the late stages, fluid resistant foot/leg covers can protect from contamination and transport.

- **Gowns or Coveralls:**

  o Fluid resistant front and back gowns are recommended. Cuffs should be snug fitting.

  o ANSI/AAMI PB70:2012 Level 4 protective gowns should be used when dealing directly with patients.

  o For exceptionally high exposure, use a Level 4 full-body suit.

  o Lesser levels may be used as standard precautions when no direct contact is required.

  o The following table lists the differing protection levels.

ANSI/AAMI PB70:2012			
Level	Description	Required	What's Better
4	ASTM F1670:Penetration by forced spray synthetic blood	Pass	Pass
4	ASTM F1671 :Bloodborne pathogen penetration: bacteriophage virus in fluid pressed through	Pass	Pass
3	AATCC 42:Spray impact – amount penetrated after fluid drop impact	<1.0g	Lower
3	AATCC 127:Hydrostatic pressure – pressure needed to force water through	$\geq$50cm	Higher
2	AATCC 42:Spray impact – amount penetrated after fluid drop impact	$\leq$1.0g	Lower
2	AATCC 127:Hydrostatic pressure – pressure needed to force water through	$\geq$20cm	Higher
1	AATCC 42:Spray impact – amount penetrated after fluid drop impact	$\leq$4.5g	Lower

- <u>Gloves</u>:

  o All gloves must be powder-free. The virus can readily contaminate powder particles and be dispersed throughout the vicinity.

  o Neither vinyl nor polyethylene gloves are appropriate for barrier protection when performing tasks with potentially infectious materials.

  o Good powder-free gloves include nitrile, natural rubber latex, polyisoprene, and neoprene. In severe situations, a medical glove beneath a thick, orthopedic-type surgical glove may be necessary.

  o If possible, double glove, making certain one glove is under the gown cuff and the other glove is over the cuff. It may be prudent to tape the glove to the cuff with duct tape to prevent the cuffs from slipping or rolling down.

  o Inner gloves should extend, at a minimum, 6" beyond the wrist.

  o Outer gloves should extend, at a minimum, 12" beyond the wrist.

  o If gloves are not available, three layers of plastic bags will suffice.

- o Reuse gloves only if supplies dictate. Check reused gloves for holes before every use. If available, put talcum powder in reusable gloves after disinfection.

- Head Covers: During later stages, virus-contaminated droplets can fall onto exposed hair. If contaminated hair is touched, hands can then become contaminated and transfer the virus to other places on the individual, or to other objects. Wearing a fluid-resistant head cover would ensure this does not occur.

- Masks:

  - o Stock N95 masks at a minimum. N95 masks should not be used for scenarios where direct contact with an infected individual is likely.

  - o If contact with an infected individual is likely, this author would wear nothing less than an N99 or N100 mask.

  - o Masks must be fluid resistant to prevent splashes from causing infection.

  - o Masks used in isolation areas should have an ASTM F2100 Level 3 designation.

  - o Level 1 and 2 masks can be used outside of isolation areas.

o The following table lists the differing protection
levels.

Maks: ASTM F2100 - Spray, Splatter, Droplet Protection		
Level	Description	Must Pass
3	ASTM F1862 Pressure spray synthetic blood: simulates high blood pressure	160mm Hg
3	ASTM 2101 Bacterial Filtration Efficiency (droplet)	≥ 98
2	ASTM F1862 Pressure spray synthetic blood: simulates normal blood pressure	120mm Hg
2	ASTM 2101 Bacterial Filtration Efficiency (droplet)	≥ 98
1	ASTM F1862 Pressure spray synthetic blood: simulates systolic blood pressure	80mm Hg
1	ASTM 2101 Bacterial Filtration Efficiency (droplet)	≥ 95

• Respirators:

o In aerosol-generating scenarios (i.e., direct
contact with an infected individual), respirators
should be worn in lieu of masks. Most
respirators require a fit test so they can be
properly sized to an individual's face.

o Men should be clean-shaven to ensure the
respirator will seal properly to their face.

o Every time a disposable respirator is worn, the
wearer must immediately perform a seal check.
This verification takes only seconds. As with
masks, respirators must also be fluid-resistant.

- o Note: Some respirators possess staples in the filtration portion of the respirator. Upon use, holes can develop where they penetrate the fabric. This may not be detected during fit tests, as the respirator has not yet been in actual use. If possible, avoid respirators of this type.

- Powered Air-Purifying Respirators (PAPR): For the best protection during extended, direct contact with an infected individual in late stages, a fit-tested half-facepiece PAPR (positive pressure), or a PAPR with a loose-fitting facepiece with a helmet or hood that does not need fit testing is advisable if available.

- Be extremely careful not to disperse contaminants during PPE removal. Assume all exposed PPE surfaces are contaminated. A designated, professionally-trained individual should assist with removal. PPEs should be immediately disinfected or disposed of.

- See the CDC poster regarding putting on and removing PPE found here:

http://www.cdc.gov/vhf/ebola/pdf/ppe-poster.pdf

Print out for future reference. Display in areas where PPEs will be removed.

- Wash hands with soap and water after PPE removal. Soap allows the virus to slip off the skin, while water carries it away. If water is not being washed into a sewer system, bleach should be added to the water until it is at a 1:10 mixture. Allow to sit for at least 10 to 15 minutes before disposal.

- Upon washing, a 70 to 90% ethyl-alcohol based hand sanitizer should be immediately applied.

- Rubbing alcohol may be used in lieu of hand sanitizer.

- Remember, the above PPE will not guarantee you will not become infected. If anything, they may grant you a sense of <u>false protection</u>. The author would envision use of such items to be in an extreme outlier scenario where medical facilities are completely overwhelmed and are no longer capable of receiving and treating patients. In such an event, if a family member is infected, you may decide to interact with them to provide care and comfort. Know that, in such a scenario, even with the above PPE, there would be a high risk of infection.

Other

- Water: Stock plenty of bottles and gallon jugs of water. Rotate your stocks regularly. Consider additional storage methods, such as 55-gallon drums (use only clean drums rated for potable water), emergency tub containers, or water bricks.

- *Water Treatment:* Stock unscented regular bleach (rotate bleach stocks regularly), iodine tablets and high-quality filtration systems (such as Berkey). Sand filters can also be integrated into your water harvesting system. Eyedroppers, activated charcoal, funnels, clean sand, gutters, rain-harvesting systems, and hand-operated pumps.

- Food (short-term): For short-term, daily use, only purchase foods that you will regularly consume, to ensure that they will not expire. Canned goods, boxed dinners, rice, noodles, peanut butter and other dry goods are all excellent options. Try to have several months (three to six) of short-term food supplies on hand.

- Food (long-term): Long-term food should be shelf stable for at least ten years. Warehouse stores (Costco, Sam's, etc.) sell five and six-gallon buckets of rice, wheat, noodles, corn meal, oatmeal, and other items that have 20 to 30-year shelf lives. They may not be sold in stores, so check online as well.

You can also do-it-yourself by purchasing food-grade buckets, Mylar bags and oxygen absorbers. Place the Mylar bags in the five-gallon buckets, fill it with dry beans or rice, add an oxygen absorber and seal the Mylar bag with a hair straightener. Finally, seal the bucket with a lid. Do not stack the buckets more than two high, to avoid damaging them. Rice and beans should last 20 to 30 years in a cool, dry place. If possible, store at least a year's supply of long-term food.

Multivitamins, honey, salt, sugar, plenty of cooking spices, Crisco, and other shelf-stable goods are also recommended.

- Food Preparation: Dehydrators, cast-iron cookware (Dutch oven, stewpot, kettles), recipe books, solar stove, meat saws, gambrels, skinning and filet knives, grain mill, grill (charcoal and propane), campfire cooking grates and a pressure cooker.

- Fuel: Charcoal, propane, matches, firewood, fuel stabilizers (for diesel and gasoline, as needed) and two-stroke mixing oil.

- <u>First Aid:</u> First-aid manual. Bandages, cloth tape, antibiotic ointment, super glue (can be used to seal a cut), antiseptic wipes, gloves, hydrocortisone ointment, scissors, gauze, floss, tweezers, eye drops, lip balm, aspirin and non-aspirin pain relievers, antacids, anti-diarrhea medicine, activated charcoal (for ingestion of poison), OTC oral antihistamines, potassium iodide tablets, cough drops, prescription medicines that do not require refrigeration, saline fluid, rubbing alcohol, hydrogen peroxide, Iodine, ammonia inhalant, Israeli bandage, sterile dressings, thermometer, petroleum jelly, burn cream, cold compress, oral pain gel, emergency oral cap repair, hand/feet warmers, CPR mouth shield, moleskin (for blisters), sewing kit, Celox (clotting agent), forceps, hemostats and anything else you deem necessary.

- <u>Oral Rehydration Solutions (ORS):</u> Keeping an infected individual hydrated is critical to their survival. Commercial options are Pedialyte and Gatorade. If commercial options are not available, make your own using:

    - 1 quart of clean water

    - 1/2 teaspoon of salt

    - 2 tablespoons honey or sugar

    - 1/2 teaspoon trisodium citrate (or baking soda)

- **Additional Information:**

Where There is no Doctor, by David Werner, et al

Where There is no Dentist, by Murray Dickson

- **Self Defense - Firearms:** At a minimum, try to outfit every member of your family who is of a responsible age with a center-fire pistol/revolver and a shotgun or center-fire rifle.

Pistols: In a disaster scenario, at a minimum, a pistol should be worn at all times, unless in a contaminated environment performing patient care. The pistol is your last line of defense, before resorting to hand combat, which you obviously want to avoid in an epidemic. Never find yourself more than a few steps away from a larger weapon, however.

For your pistols, choose established brands and models and try to outfit everyone with the same caliber and model. Your pistol caliber should be, at a minimum, a 9mm or .38 Special. If that means you are forced to adopt 9mm because two or three members of your group are unable to accurately use a larger caliber, then do it. Imagine having six members of your family outfitted with Glock 19 pistols (9mm) and spare parts for them. You would need to purchase only one type of ammunition. Spare parts and magazines would be interchangeable. Also, everyone could train in the same fashion.

Alex Smith

Shotgun: The shotgun is the jack-of-all-trades firearm. Good for harvesting small game (with birdshot), large game and self-defense (buckshot), out to 25 or 30 yards. The shotgun's effective range can be extended to 75 or 100 yards with the use of slugs. The shotgun can fill many roles, but is seldom ever the best option available. What it *is*, is an effective, low-cost weapon that is rugged and dependable.

Pump-action shotguns such as the Mossberg 500/590 and Remington 870 are tried and true weapons. The author is particularly biased towards these two models because of the sheer number of aftermarket accessories available for them. Stick to 12 and/or 20-gauge shotguns. If a large portion of your family is uncomfortable with a 12 gauge's recoil, opting for a full line of 20 gauge models would be acceptable. Splitting between these two gauges would also be acceptable.

Center-fire Rifle: Center-fire rifles protect your life and liberty from those that would do you harm – that is their primary goal. If large-game harvesting (but not during an epidemic) is a secondary goal in your location, choose a larger caliber, such as a .308. Otherwise:

If you choose a military-style weapon for this platform, it is hard to go wrong. If budget permits, a magazine-fed, semi-automatic rifle such as the AR-15 in 5.56mm/.223 is an excellent choice. (Note: an AR rated for 5.56mm can also fire .223, but .223 rifles may not necessarily shoot 5.56mm – because of higher pressures. Check with the manufacturer to be certain.) AR-15s are becoming more and more ubiquitous, and the aftermarket options are vast. AKMs (AK-47, MAK-90, etc.) in 7.62x39mm are also rugged weapons, but their price has been steadily rising over the years. As the price of ARs fall and AKs rise, the price difference between the two is becoming minimal. Ultimately, buy what you prefer.

- <u>Communications:</u> Ham radio, CB radios (in vehicles and handheld), FRS handhelds, emergency radio, batteries, rechargeable batteries, battery charger and a police scanner.

- <u>Planting/Gardening:</u> Seeds, fertilizer, wheelbarrow, non-electric cultivator (visit Lehman's for non-electric gardening tools), greenhouse building supplies and plenty of seeding cups and pots. <u>This is not so much for during an epidemic, but for afterwards. An epidemic would wreak havoc on a Just-in-Time (JIT) economy.</u>

- <u>Building Supplies:</u> Plywood, lumber, PVC pipe, fencing supplies, hardware (nails, screws, hinges, bolts, nuts, glues, adhesives, caulks, etc.), etc.

- <u>Games:</u> Board games, playing cards, books for all ages, coloring supplies, pens, pencils, notebooks, horseshoes, dart boards, sports gear, etc.

- <u>Sanitation/Hygiene:</u> Hand sanitizer, soap (all kinds – hand, dish, laundry, etc.), deodorant, toothpaste, toothbrushes, floss, mouthwash, brushes, combs, female sanitation products, grooming supplies (clippers, scissors, tweezers, files, fingernail brushes, etc.), sunscreen, anti-fungal spray, condoms, toilet paper, paper towels, hand towels, bleach, disinfectants (Lysol, ammonia-based products, alcohol and vinegar), lime (for outhouses during a sustained epidemic), garbage bags, mops, mop buckets, brooms, dustpan, scrubbing pads, clothesline kits, and rags.

Closing

I hope this book has been of use to you. Share it with your family and neighbors as needed. May you never need the information contained herein.

"Fortune favors the prepared mind." --Louis Pasteur